S

SACRAMENTO PUBLIC LIBRARY

Foundation

Dear Parent:
Your child's love of reading starts here!

Every child learns to read in a different way and at his or her own speed. Some go back and forth between reading levels and read favorite books again and again. Others read through each level in order. You can help your young reader improve and become more confident by encouraging his or her own interests and abilities. From books your child reads with you to the first books he or she reads alone, there are I Can Read Books for every stage of reading:

SHARED READING
Basic language, word repetition, and whimsical illustrations, ideal for sharing with your emergent reader

BEGINNING READING
Short sentences, familiar words, and simple concepts for children eager to read on their own

READING WITH HELP
Engaging stories, longer sentences, and language play for developing readers

READING ALONE
Complex plots, challenging vocabulary, and high-interest topics for the independent reader

ADVANCED READING
Short paragraphs, chapters, and exciting themes for the perfect bridge to chapter books

I Can Read Books have introduced children to the joy of reading since 1957. Featuring award-winning authors and illustrators and a fabulous cast of beloved characters, I Can Read Books set the standard for beginning readers.

A lifetime of discovery begins with the magical words "I Can Read!"

Visit www.icanread.com for information
on enriching your child's reading experience.

For Liz Graves

I Can Read Book® is a trademark of HarperCollins Publishers.

Santa's Moose
Copyright © 1979 by Syd Hoff
All rights reserved. Manufactured in China.
No part of this book may be used or reproduced in any manner whatsoever without written permission except
in the case of brief quotations embodied in critical articles and reviews. For information address HarperCollins
Children's Books, a division of HarperCollins Publishers, 195 Broadway, New York, NY 10007.
www.icanread.com

ISBN 978-0-06-246308-7 (trade bdg.) — ISBN 978-0-06-264307-0 (pbk.)

Book design by Rick Farley

17 18 19 20 21 SCP 10 9 8 7 6 5 4 3 2 1   ❖   First Edition

I Can Read!™

BEGINNING READING 1

SANTA'S MOOSE

by Syd Hoff

HARPER

An Imprint of HarperCollinsPublishers

It was winter in the forest.

"Soon Christmas will be here,"

said Milton the moose.

Birds landed

on Milton's antlers

to rest,

then flew south.

The animals put holly leaves

on their nests and caves.

"We're on our way

to help Santa Claus,"

said eight little reindeer.

"That sounds like fun,"

said Milton.

He ran after the reindeer.

"May I please help
pull your sleigh?" asked Milton.

"I have never used a moose before,

but I'm willing

if you are," said Santa.

And across the sky they flew.

The eight little reindeer

liked Milton.

It was easy

to pull the heavy sleigh

with a big moose to help.

But Milton did not know

how to land on a roof.

KERPLUNK!

went Milton's big feet.

"Hush, you will wake everyone,"

said Santa.

Milton did not know

Santa went down chimneys alone.

He tried to go down too.

"You will get stuck," said Santa.

Milton waited

with the reindeer.

But he wanted to see

Santa fill the stockings

and put presents

around the Christmas tree.

He leaned over the roof

to peek,

and down he fell.

"I guess I should go home.

I guess I will never be good

at this," Milton said.

"Yes you will," said the reindeer.

"None of us were good
in the beginning."
"All it takes is practice,"
said Santa. "Please stay."

So Milton flew

all over the world

with Santa and

the eight little reindeer.

He learned to land on a roof.

He learned to stand still
and wait for Santa,
even when it took him
a long time.

At one house,

Santa let Milton

and the reindeer

stay on the ground.

Milton watched Santa

put presents

under the Christmas tree

and candy in the stockings.

"Christmas is the best time
of the year!" said Milton.
But the little reindeer were tired.
"We cannot go another step,"
they said.

"The load is so heavy this year!

But if we stop

there will be no presents

for millions of children."

"Do not stop!" cried Milton.

"I can pull the sleigh by myself."

Milton flew ahead.

The eight little reindeer

glided after him.

All the toys were delivered.

"Thank you, Milton,"

the reindeer said.

"We could not have done it

without you," said Santa.

"Will you help us next year?"

"Of course," said Milton.

"Merry Christmas!" said Santa.

"Merry Christmas!" cried the reindeer.

Santa and the reindeer

flew back to the North Pole.

Milton went back to the forest.

"Merry Christmas, everyone!"

he said.

He thought of Santa.

He thought of

the eight little reindeer.

He thought of next year,

when he would help them again.

"Joy to the world," he said,

"and peace on earth!"